DISCOVER
AMAZING ANIMALS

Copyright: North Parade Publishing Ltd.
3-6 Henrietta Mews,
Bath BA2 6LR. UK

This edition: 2024

Predominant artwork and imagery source: Shutterstock.
Additional images: Mary Swift

All rights reserved. No part of this publication may be reprinted, stored in a retrieval system or transmitted in any form or by any means, electronic, mechanical, photocopying, recording, or otherwise, without the prior permission of the copyright holder.

Contents

Animal Kingdom	6
Animals of North America	8
Animals of South America	10
Animals of Africa	12
Animals of Australia	14
Animals of Asia	16
Animals of Europe	18
Animals of the Arctic and Antarctic Regions	20
Splendid Reptiles	22
Amazing Amphibians	24
Magnificent Mammals	26
The Big Cats	28
Mighty Bears	30
Primates	32
Ocean Dwellers – Sharks	34
Ocean Dwellers – Cetaceans	36
Extinct Animals	38
Prehistoric Creatures (Marine)	40
Prehistoric Creatures (Terrestrial)	42
Prehistoric Creatures (Dinosaurs)	44

Animal Kingdom

All the creatures we see around us – ranging from bugs, birds, fish, mammals, reptiles, sharks, whales – all come under the category of "animals". The animal kingdom is vast, with millions of species.

The two main groups in the animal kingdom are: vertebrates (those that have a backbone) and invertebrates (those without a backbone).

Annelids: are segmented worms that are found in different wet environments and include creatures such as leeches and earthworms.

Invertebrates

Invertebrates make up the largest group in the animal kingdom, accounting for nearly 97 percent of all animals. All insects, worms, sponges, jellyfish, squids, snails, leeches, and starfish come under invertebrates. They range in size from microscopic dust mites to the 18-metre-long giant squid, the largest invertebrate in the world! About 1.25 million species of invertebrates have been identified so far, though the numbers could be as high as 30 million. Compare this to merely 30,000 vertebrate species!

Types of invertebrates

- Protozoa
- Platyhelminthes
- Nematodes
- Cnidaria
- Annelids
- Echinodermata
- Molluscs
- Arthropods

Cnidaria: making up over 9,000 species, cnidarians include marine animals such as jellyfish, corals, hydra, sea anemones, sea pens and more.

Arthropods: arthropods include small land insects such as spiders and larger marine animals such as lobsters and crabs.

Platyhelminthes: also called flatworms, they are free-living or parasitic worms that have flat bodies with no segments.

Nematodes: they make up a class of small and slender worms, some of which are microscopic while others reach up to 1 metre in length!

Molluscs: these soft-bodied animals are covered in thick shells.

Protozoa: this is a group of single-celled eukaryotic microbes, many of which are parasites and cause diseases.

Vertebrates

Vertebrates have a bony skeleton (also known as backbone) that gives them structure and support. Even though the bony skeleton is the most prominent feature in vertebrates now, the early vertebrates had only a notochord – a primitive, flexible rod that plays a role in the development of the nervous system. The common categories of vertebrates are: reptiles, amphibians, fish, birds and mammals.

Mammals

Mammals are vertebrates that give birth to young ones and feed them milk. The milk-producing glands are known as mammary glands. Though most mammals live on land, some are aquatic (whales) or semi-aquatic (otters).

Birds

These feathered vertebrates have features of both reptiles and mammals, though they are more closely related to reptiles. They have forelimbs modified into wings, good vision and lay eggs out of which the young birds hatch. Even though almost all birds are capable of flight, there are exceptions. Flightless birds include ostrich, emu, kiwi and penguin.

Fish

Fish range in length from about a centimetre to nearly 20 metres. Apart from bony fish, the oceans and freshwater bodies are home to many varieties of rays, sharks and skates. Fish often lay hundreds or thousands of eggs, though very few survive. Fish breathe through special structures called gills.

Reptiles

Reptiles are cold-blooded animals which were dominant millions of years ago during the Mesozoic Era - also referred to as the golden age of reptiles. The most fascinating reptiles – the dinosaurs – thrived during this period. The reptiles today include crocodiles, turtles, tortoises, snakes, lizards and tuataras. They are covered in scales or tough bony plates and lay eggs with tough shells.

Amphibians

Amphibians are adapted for surviving in water as well as on land though the eggs often hatch in water. Frogs and toads are the most prominent among the amphibians.

Animals of North America

North America is a vast area covering Canada, the United States, Greenland and Mexico. It includes a variety of mountains, plains and lowlands and unique habitats and climates and, as a result, is home to a variety of wildlife species.

Location
North America has a wide range of habitats and rich diversity in terms of flora and fauna. There are grasslands, forests, meadows and major mountain ranges such as the Rocky Mountains and Sierra Nevada.

American alligator
American alligators, the largest reptiles in North America, are quite similar to crocodiles but have a round snout, flat tail and short legs. They can have up to 75 to 80 teeth that are replaced whenever they fall out or wear. Even though alligators mainly feed on fish, birds and other small animals, occasionally they've also been spotted eating berries, citrus fruits and wild grapes!

Size: 3 to 4.5 metres; Weight: 1,000 lbs / 450 kg

Raccoon
With their characteristic eye masks and ringed tails, raccoons are a remarkably clever and adaptable animal that thrive well in the wild and in urban areas! They have very high sensitivity to touch and can guess an object just by touching it. Did you know that Toronto in Canada is the raccoon capital of the world? Fifty times more raccoons reside here than in the wild. The black fur around their eyes reduces glare and helps them see well.

Size: 40 to 70 centimetres; Weight: 14 to 23 lbs / 6 to 10 kg

Groundhog
A groundhog is a rodent that looks like a giant squirrel that lives in burrows in the ground. Two funny nicknames for a groundhog are "woodchuck" and "whistlepig". A groundhog can build an amazing burrow that can be anything from 2.4 to 20 metres long and have many chambers and exits. Every year, as a tradition, groundhogs are used to predict weather in America.

Size: 42 to 68.5 centimetres; Weight: 13 lbs / 6 kg

American bison
The American bison is the largest mammal in North America. At one time, there were millions of them roaming the landscape, but overhunting has destroyed most of the population, with only around 50,000 bison remaining in the wild. Its thick furry brown coat and towering hump and short, curvy horns are its characteristic features.

Size: 1.8 metres; Weight: 2,000 lbs / 900 kg

Black carpenter ant

Black carpenter ants are common in the Rocky Mountain ranges and eastern Canada and have a notorious reputation for destroying trees and wooden structures. Unlike termites, these ants don't feed on wood – rather, they bore through the wood making tunnel-like galleries. These ants spray formic acid after biting that can cause a stinging sensation!

Size: 0.6 to 1.2 centimetres;
Weight: less than 10 milligrams

Luna moth

Native to America, luna moths have bright green wings. Interestingly, they do not have a mouth or a digestive system. In fact, after turning into moths, they only live for about a week and don't eat anything at all. Luna moths are one of the larger moth species found in North America. They camouflage themselves well amidst leaf clusters and are often found in woodlands.

Size: Wingspan - 8 to 11.5 centimetres;
Weight: Average 0.3 to 0.4 grams

Bighorn sheep

Bighorn sheep are found across a large range stretching from the Rocky Mountains to the American Southwest. Their best known feature is their large, stout, curvy horns. When the rams fight, they rear up and hurl at each other – often repeatedly. Their fights can last for hours. Ouch! Their thick skulls prevent them from sustaining any serious injury.

Size: 1.5 to 1.8 metres;
Weight: 115 to 280 lbs / 50 to 125 kg

Gila monster

Gila monsters are the largest and only venomous lizards found in the United States. Despite their name, they are neither gigantic in size, nor do they attack ferociously. This reptile is known for its sluggish nature. It has beaded scales and pink, yellow or orange patterns on its body.

Size: 50 centimetres; Weight: 4 lbs / 2 kg

Bald eagle

A bald eagle's most prominent feature is its snowy white feathers on its head and tail. The largest population of bald eagles are found in Alaska and Canada. They have excellent eyesight and use their powerful talons to grab fish and small animals by diving down at a speed of about 160 kilometres per hour. A bald eagle's nest can be up to 3 metres in diameter and 6 metres deep!

Size: 86 to 109 centimetres; Weight: 6.5 to 14 lbs / 3 to 6 kg

Animals of South America

South America is the home of the Andes Mountains, the Amazon River and the tropical forest region around the river basin. In fact, the Amazon rainforest exhibits amazing diversity, and millions of different species live here!

Location
This southern continent is roughly triangular in shape and is home to deserts, grasslands, mountains, lush tropical vegetation, many rivers and lakes and is surrounded by ocean all around.

Chinchilla
Chinchillas are rodents that live in the Andes. A chinchilla looks like a rabbit with short ears and has a bushy tail and thick, velvety fur that provides great warmth in the cold mountains where it lives. Its fur is so soft that it is nearly 30 times softer than human hair. In the wild, chinchillas live in small or big herds!

Size: 22 to 49 centimetres; Weight: 0.8 to 3 lbs / 0.3 to 1.3 kg

Llama
A llama is a South American camel species covered in thick fur and lacking a hump. Llamas have been domesticated and used as pack animals for hundreds of years in the Andes Mountains. An overloaded llama will simply refuse to move! They may even spit or hiss to show their disapproval. They make excellent guards, taking care of sheep and small animals much like guard dogs!

Size: 1.2 metres; Weight: 250 lbs / 115 kg

Capybara
Capybaras are the largest rodents in the world! They are semi-aquatic and excellent swimmers and divers. A capybara can even sleep in water keeping just its nose on the river bank. It feeds on grass, aquatic plants and often its own dung for additional nutrition.

Size: 1.4 metres; Weight: 77 to 143 lbs / 35 to 65 kg

Armadillo
The name "armadillo" means "the little armoured one" in Spanish. An armadillo has prominent armour-like plates on its body and sharp claws for digging. It is closely related to anteaters. Did you know that an armadillo always gives birth to quadruplets, each exactly alike? When an armadillo is startled or threatened, it can jump up more than a metre high in the air!

Size: 76 centimetres; Weight: 12 lbs / 5.5 kg

Green anaconda

The green anaconda is the largest and heaviest snake in the world! An anaconda is nonpoisonous but it can catch a prey by coiling and squeezing hard until the animal dies of asphyxiation. It also swallows its prey whole, sometimes going weeks, or even months, without eating again after a single big meal!

Size: 6 to 9 metres; Weight: 500 to 550 lbs / 225 to 250 kg

Howler monkey

A howler monkey is easily the loudest among monkeys! They usually call out to other monkeys to mark their territory! They live in trees, feeding on fruits, flowers and leaves and usually get all the water they need from them. They have prehensile tails capable of gripping a branch.

Size: 0.6 to 1.2 metres; Weight: 22 lbs / 10kg

Pink river dolphin

Also called "boto" and "bufeo", this freshwater dolphin species is found in the Amazon River. It got its name from the pink skin colour of male dolphins. The pink river dolphin is not only the largest among river dolphins, but also the smartest! Unlike other dolphins, they have a swollen forehead and a long beak!

Size: 2.4 metres; Weight: 450 lbs / 205 kg

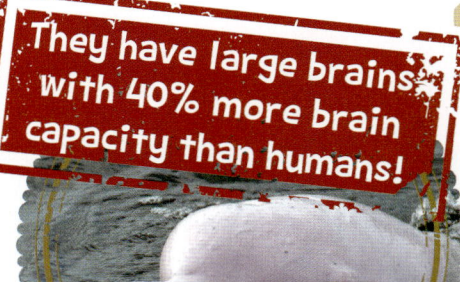

They have large brains with 40% more brain capacity than humans!

Piranha

Piranhas, with their razor-sharp teeth, have a reputation for vicious attacks and aggressive feeding frenzy, but this is largely exaggerated by people and in movies! While they may feed on the carcass of a larger animal, they usually feed on smaller fish, worms and other marine creatures. In fact, some piranha species are vegetarian. The word "piranha" actually means "tooth fish".

Size: up to 60 centimetres; Weight: 6.5 lbs / 3 kg

Sloth

A sloth is famous for its sluggish nature — spending most of its time hanging from a branch and sleeping for up to 18 hours a day! But did you know that they can move three times faster in water than on land? A sloth can hold its breath for up to 40 minutes underwater! A sloth's fur is often covered in algae. This gives them excellent camouflage.

Size: 58 to 68 centimetres; Weight: 17.5 to 18.75 lbs / 8 to 8.5 kg

Poison dart frog

A poison dart frog lives in the Amazon rainforest and is brightly coloured — usually bright blue or yellow with black markings. Interestingly, this famously poisonous frog is not poisonous in a zoo, under a controlled diet. In the wild, the frogs produce their poison by feeding on poisonous ants and insects! The parents often carry their tadpoles on their back across the forest to transport them to water!

Size: 20 to 40 millimetres; Weight: 0.06 lbs / 30 grams

Animals of Africa

Africa is the hottest continent in the world with large deserts like the Sahara and Kalahari as well as adjoining grasslands known as savannah. This second largest continent is home to animals such as the African elephant, zebra, giraffe, lion, cheetah and many others!

Location
Africa is the second-largest continent in the world and one of the most diverse places on the planet in terms of climate and vegetation, with forests, wetlands, grasslands and the large Sahara Desert and different species residing in all types of habitats.

Ostrich
Found in the African savannahs, the ostrich is the world's largest bird. It has a long neck, a bulky body and powerful legs. An ostrich can run at a speed of 70 kilometres per hour! The legs don't just help with the running – they are also useful for self-defense. An ostrich can deliver a powerful kick to predators such as hyena or cheetah. An ostrich egg can measure 15 centimetres and weigh 3 lbs (1.5 kg).

Size: 2.1 to 2.7 metres; Weight: 330 to 350 lbs / 150 to 160 kg

Spotted hyena
A spotted hyena has a ginger coat with black spots. Even though these hyenas are expert hunters, they don't mind eating leftover carcasses. When hunting in groups, they can easily overpower a young hippo or antelope. It's called a laughing hyena because when it whoops or yells, it sounds like person cackling.

Size: up to 2 metres; Weight: 110 to 190 lbs / 50 to 85 kg

Picasso bug
A close relative of the stink bug, the pretty Picasso bug can release an unpleasant odour if disturbed. It feeds almost entirely on plant juices. It is mainly found in cotton, citrus and coffee plants.

Size: 6 to 8 millimetres

Meerkat
Belonging to the mongoose family, meerkats live in large groups in burrows with multiple entrances. They easily tackle poisonous millipedes and scorpions and feed on them. Meerkats are very cooperative – a small group of meerkats called "sentry" stay guard while the others eat. This little mammal is most well-known for its ability to stand upright!

Size: 29 centimetres; Weight: 720 to 730 grams

Warthog

Warthogs are related to pigs but look different. A warthog has a flat head covered in protective warts or bumps and has four sharp tusks that it uses for attacking. Warthogs appear aggressive but prefer running to attacking. They can run at a speed of 48 kilometres per hour. Did you know that a warthog can go for months without water if needed?

Size: 76 centimetres;
Weight: 120 to 250 lbs / 55 to 115 kg

Black rhinoceros

Of the five rhino species, two are found in Africa and the black rhinoceros is the smaller of the two. It is a bulky animal with a square lip and two tough horns. It is currently an endangered species, with only about 5,600 around as of 2020. Despite the name, a black rhino is actually grey in colour. Rhinos love wallowing in mud: it helps protect them from bugs and acts as a natural sunscreen.

Size: 2.5 to 4 metres;
Weight: 1,750 to 3,000 lbs / 800 to 1,350 kg

Black mamba

The black mamba is the longest venomous snake in Africa. They are highly aggressive when threatened. Black mambas are olive green or grey in colour and get their name from the blue-black colour of the inside portion of their mouth. They are among the fastest snakes, capable of slithering at a speed of 20 kilometres per hour.

Size: 4.2 metres;
Weight: 3.5 lbs / 1.5 kg

Black Mambas strike repeatedly and have black mouths

Giraffe

The giraffe is the world's tallest mammal. A giraffe's leg alone is taller than many humans, measuring nearly 2 metres. Its height allows it to feed on leaves from treetops and keep a lookout for predators. A giraffe is most vulnerable when it drinks water, as it has to spread its legs apart and stretch its neck down. However, it needs to drink only once in a few days as it gets most of its water from the leaves it eats. A giraffe's heart is big and weighs 25 lbs (11 kg) so that it can pump blood all the way along its long neck to the brain!

Size: 4.6 to 6.1 metres; Weight: 1,750 to 2,800 lbs / 800 to 1,250 kg

Animals of Australia

Australia is home to some unique animal species not found anywhere else in the world! Marsupials, a class of mammals that have a pouch to carry and nurse their young ones in, are found almost exclusively in Australia.

Koala

Koalas are often called 'koala bears' though they don't belong to the bear family. Their round ears and black noses are their characteristic features. They feed almost exclusively on eucalyptus leaves (about a kilo of leaves in a day) which are poisonous to most other animals. The leaves are also low in nutrition, so to conserve energy, a koala sleeps for up to 18 hours a day!

Size: 60 – 80 centimetres; Weight: 20 lbs / 9 kg

Location

This continent lies in the Southern Hemisphere between the Pacific and Indian Oceans. As a geographically isolated country, the animals found here are very different from those elsewhere!

Redback spider

A redback spider is the Australian cousin of the black widow spider. It has a characteristic red marking on its body. It's a venomous spider that can deliver a bite with its fangs that can be painful and very dangerous. It can catch and feed on insects much larger than itself!

Size: 3 millimetres (male) – 1 centimetre (female)

Tasmanian devil

A Tasmanian devil has brown or black fur and looks like a dog and is the biggest carnivorous marsupial in the world. They earned the name 'devils' when early European settlers found that they could turn fierce, bare teeth, growl and lunge when threatened!

Size: 50 to 78 centimetres; Weight: 9 to 26 lbs / 4 to 12 kg

Kangaroos and wallabies

Kangaroos and wallabies are marsupials that have strong hind legs useful for hopping swiftly. They can also walk slowly on four legs. The red kangaroo is the largest marsupial in the world. Baby kangaroos and wallabies are called joeys. A kangaroo can not only hop with their powerful hind legs but also deliver punches to their predators!

Size: 1 to 1.6 metres; Weight: 200 lbs / 90 kg

Echidna

Like the platypus, an echidna is also an egg-laying mammal. It is also known as spiny anteater. It has spines like a porcupine and a long snout like an anteater. They open logs with their claws and use their long tongue to scoop termites, ants and beetle larvae. An echidna lays only one egg at a time and a baby echidna is called a "puggle".

Size: 30 to 43 centimetres; *Weight:* 4 to 10 lbs / 2 to 4.5 kg

Wombat

A wombat looks like a cuddly baby bear and generally walks with a waddle, but don't be deceived! It can run at a speed of 25 miles per hour if needed. Wombats are also expert diggers, capable of making complex tunnels and chambers underground with their long claws. Wombats are the only animals in the world whose poop is cube-shaped!

Size: 71 to 120 centimetres; *Weight:* 32 to 80 lbs / 14 to 36 kg

Emu

Emu is the second largest bird after the ostrich. Did you know that it lays green eggs? An emu cannot fly, but it can run fast – really fast, clocking speeds of 50 kilometres per hour. That's much faster than Usain Bolt! Emus have a powerful but low-pitched voice that can be heard up to 2 kilometres away.

Size: 1.6 to 1.8 metres; *Weight:* 66 to 100 lbs / 30 to 45 kg

Responsible for most deaths by snakebite in Australia

Eastern brown snake

The eastern brown snake is not only one of the most venomous and aggressive snakes, but also one of the fastest! It is found in the eastern region of Australia. It can range in colour from tan to deep brown to black, with a lighter underside.

Length: over 2 metres

Platypus

A platypus is one of the oddest animals you'll find. It has the beak and webbed feet of a duck, the body and fur of an otter, the tail of a beaver and it lays eggs! Not surprisingly, when a sketch of this animal was sent to Britain, the scientists thought it was a hoax!

Size: 38 centimetres; *Weight:* 3 lbs / 1.5 kg

Animals of Asia

Asia is the largest continent and exhibits great diversity in its habitats. Despite its densely populated urban areas, there are also jungles and forests in Asia with thousands of species.

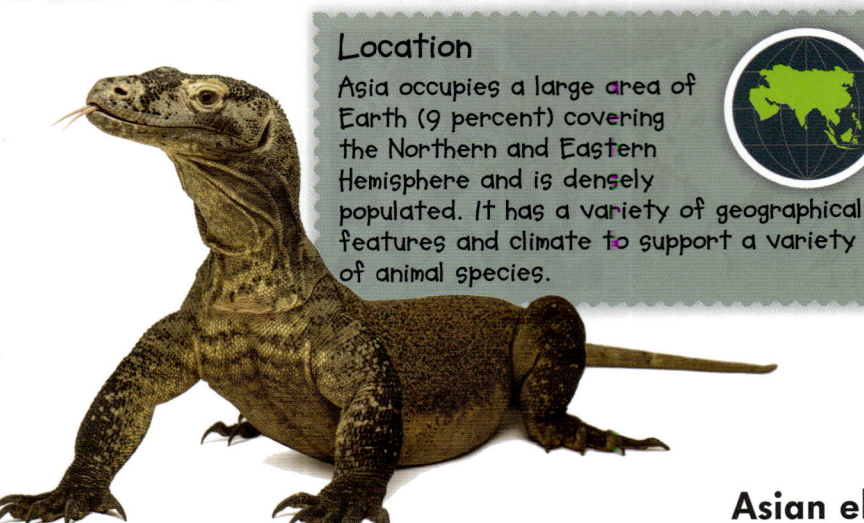

Location
Asia occupies a large area of Earth (9 percent) covering the Northern and Eastern Hemisphere and is densely populated. It has a variety of geographical features and climate to support a variety of animal species.

Komodo dragon
The komodo dragon is the heaviest, largest lizard species alive today. A komodo dragon has been known to feed on their own offspring when hungry. Until they grow up, young komodo dragons learn to climb trees or even roll in dung to appear unappetizing to hungry adults! They have forked tongues, like snakes, to smell and hunt for their food.

Size: 3 metres; Weight: 330 lbs / 150 kg

Asian elephant
The Asian elephant is the largest land animal. Its characteristic feature is its long trunk – like an extended nose – which it uses for smelling, drinking, grabbing a meal, and trumpeting! An elephant's trunk contains 100,000 different muscles. Elephants are very intelligent and have excellent memory. Male elephants have prominent tusks. There are only 20,000 to 40,000 elephants left in the wild.

Size: 2 to 3 metres; Weight: 4,500 to 11,000 lbs / 2,000 to 5,000 kg

Giant panda
While sloths or koalas spend a good part of the day sleeping, giant pandas spend most of their time eating. A panda spends 10 to 16 hours eating bamboo – its favourite food. While bamboo is its main food, it occasionally eats eggs, fish or small animals.

Size: 1.2 to 1.5 metres; Weight: 155 to 275 lbs / 70 to 125 kg

Red panda
A red panda is very different from its giant cousin and looks more like a fox! It has a thick, bushy ringed tail like a raccoon that it wraps around its body to protect it from cold, high altitude habitats. It spends most of its life in trees. Though it is fond of bamboo, it includes a variety of food in its diet including acorns, roots, fruits and eggs.

Size: 58 centimetres; Weight: 6 to 13 lbs / 3 to 6 kg

Gliding lizards

These lizards, found in the rainforests in India and southeast Asia, have wing flaps supported by elongated ribs that help them glide across trees. They spend most of their lives in trees and their diet mainly consists of ants and termites. In a single glide, a flying lizard can travel up to 8 metres and it glides not just to hunt for food, but also to chase rivals away from the trees that it claims as its own!

Size: 19.5 to 21.2 centimetres; Weight: 0.04 – 0.046 lbs / 18 to 20 grams

Tarsier

A tarsier is the second smallest primate on the planet. It has large eyes, a prominent feature of its small body. Tarsiers are found in the forests in Southeast Asia. Their tails are about twice the length of their body! They have digit-like paws with adhesive pads which make it easy to cling to trees.

Size: 15 centimetres; Weight: 30 to 160 grams

Orangutan

The word "orangutan" means "human of the forest". An orangutan is our closest relative! Orangutans live in trees and are solitary creatures. They have really long arms, longer than their body length. An orangutan is the largest tree-dwelling mammal in the world. They make comfortable nests or platforms to rest in.

Size: 1.2 to 1.5 metres; Weight: 73 to 180 lbs / 33 to 80 kg

Peacock

Peacocks and peafowls are found in India, Sri Lanka, Java and Myanmar. Male peachicks don't grow their train of attractive tail feathers until they reach the age of three! Despite the heavy tail feathers, these birds can fly quite efficiently. Did you know that a peacock sheds its feathers every year after the mating season?

Size: 30 centimetres (100 to 115 centimetres including tail feathers); Weight: 8 to 13 lbs / 3.5 to 6 kg

Female mantises have a reputation for eating males after mating

Orchid mantis

An orchid mantis is a praying mantis species that looks exactly like a pink orchid. When it rests on a leaf, it rocks gently to imitate a flower, thus escaping from predators. They also secrete chemicals called "pheromones" which attract insects towards them, which they feed upon.

Size: 6 centimetres; Weight: 28 grams

Animals of Europe

Europe is a continent that is rich in natural vegetation with a moderate climate. Virgin forests, meadows, steppes, moors and wetlands make up a good part of the continent enabling a variety of animal species to thrive here!

Location

Europe is a continent located in the Northern Hemisphere and includes island countries like Iceland and UK. Europe mostly experiences a cool, temperate climate with polar climate in the north and subtropical climate in the south.

Alpine ibex

The alpine ibex is a mountain goat native to the Alpine Mountains. Its most prominent feature is its massive curved horns. In winter, its coat is greyish brown whereas in summer it is reddish brown. They can climb steep mountain slopes with ease and jump 1.8 metres without a running start!

Size: 149 to 171 centimetres;
Weight: 150 to 260 lbs / 68 to 118 kg

Eurasian lynx

The Eurasian lynx is the rarest and most secretive among the big cats. A very distinctive feature of the Eurasian lynx, not seen in the other species, is the black tufts in its ears. It has a coat with dark spots. It operates so secretively that it is difficult to spot or even know about its presence. After the brown bear and wolf, it is the largest predator in Europe.

Size: 80 to 130 centimetres;
Weight: 84 to 99 lbs / 38 to 45 kg

Atlantic puffin

A puffin looks like a penguin but has a colourful beak. Not surprisingly, it has often been referred to as "sea parrot". Puffins are excellent swimmers and divers and spend most of their lives in the sea. Iceland is where nearly 60 percent of puffins arrive to lay their eggs and rear their young. They feed on small fish like herrings and sand eels.

Size: 25 centimetres;
Weight: 0.44 lbs / 200 grams

Common adder

The common adder, also called the black adder, is the only poisonous snake native to Britain. The word "adder" is an old English term for serpent. These snakes are usually plain black or have zigzag markings on their backs. After biting its prey, the adder releases it and later tracks it using its sense of smell.

Size: 60 to 90 centimetres;
Weight: 0.1 to 0.3 lbs / 45 to 135 grams

Mute swan

This large bird has a graceful curved neck and an orange bill with a black knob. Despite its name, a mute swan is capable of making grunting sounds and low whistles, but is less noisy than the other swan species. Swans are aggressively territorial, and hiss and scare away intruders arriving in their territory.

Size: 140 to 160 centimetres;
Weight: 22 to 26 lbs / 10 to 12 kg

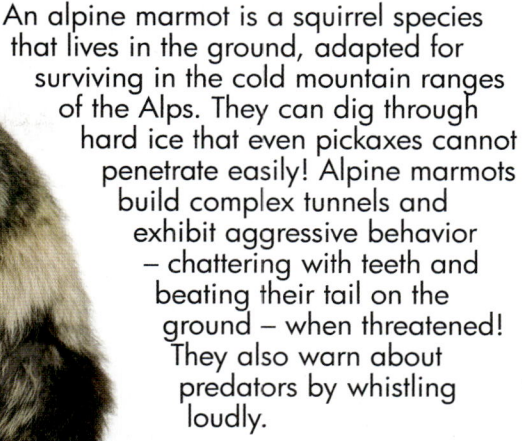

Alpine marmot

An alpine marmot is a squirrel species that lives in the ground, adapted for surviving in the cold mountain ranges of the Alps. They can dig through hard ice that even pickaxes cannot penetrate easily! Alpine marmots build complex tunnels and exhibit aggressive behavior – chattering with teeth and beating their tail on the ground – when threatened! They also warn about predators by whistling loudly.

Size: 42 to 54 centimetres;
Weight: 4.2 to 17.6 lbs / 2 to 8 kg

Hedgehog

The hedgehog is named so because it often roots through hedges hunting for food and makes pig-like grunting sounds. It has a coat of sharp spines and curls up into a ball when threatened by a predator. A hedgehog can have anything from 5000 to 7000 quills on its back! They rely on their sense of smell because they have poor eyesight and hearing.

Size: 12 to 30 centimetres; Weight: 0.8 to 2.4 lbs / 0.4 to 1 kg

Easily identified by their upright ear tufts and orange eyes

Eurasian eagle owl

Among the largest owls in the world, the Eurasian eagle-owls are capable of powerful gliding and flights. They can soar like hawks and have prominent tufted ears, feathered talons and pumpkin orange-coloured eyes. They are very adaptable, living in a variety of habitats ranging from hot deserts to cool coniferous forests.

Size: 58 to 71 centimetres; Weight: 6 lbs / 2.75 kg

Reindeer

Reindeer are large-sized deer species with prominent antlers. Did you know that reindeer have really special noses? The nose of a reindeer warms up the frigid cold air before it is sent to its lungs! Reindeer hooves are special, too! They expand in the summer and shrink in the winter. A reindeer's favourite food is lichens, a type of moss, so much so that it is called reindeer moss.

Size: 1.2 metres tall; Weight: 240 to 700 lbs / 108 to 318 kg

Animals of the Arctic and Antarctic Regions

The Arctic region and it counterpart in the south, the Antarctic region, are the coldest parts of the world that receive less sunlight and are almost always covered in frost. The vegetation is sparse here and only few animals and birds with special adaptations survive here.

Emperor penguin

Of the 17 species of penguins, the emperor penguin is the largest and the only species that lives in the icy landscape of Antarctica. An adult penguin grows as tall as a six-year-old! They have fat deposits in the body and layers of scale-like feathers to protect them from the icy cold winds. Newly hatched penguin chicks would die within minutes if not for the warmth of the mother penguin's brood pouch.

Size: 1.1 metres; Weight: up to 88 lbs / 40 kg

Snowy owl

While most owls hunt during the night, snowy owls are active during the day. They have excellent eyesight but that might not be enough to see tiny animals in, or buried under, the snow. This is where its keen sense of hearing comes in useful. It patiently waits and listens while seated on low posts and quickly snatches its prey with sharp talons!

Size: 116 to 165 centimetres; Weight: 3.5 to 6.5 lbs / 1.5 to 3 kg

Location

Antarctica is the world's southernmost continent and is where the geographic south pole is located. Once a part of the supercontinent Gondwana, it broke away about 25 million years ago. It is one of the coldest continents on Earth and is mostly a frozen desert.

Walrus

A walrus's characteristic features are its whiskers, bulky body, flat flippers and long tusks. With a body filled with oily blubber, walruses easily manage in the chilly Arctic climate and icy waters. They can slow down their heartbeat enough to endure the cold temperatures. They use their tusks for different purposes including defence, breaking ice, or showing dominance.

Size: 3.6 metres;
Weight: up to 3,000 lbs / 1,360 kg

Arctic hare

Arctic hares have snow white coloured fur in winter to give them good camouflage from predators. In the warmer months, they have bluish grey fur that blends well with the rocks and vegetation. Arctic hares can stand on their hind legs to spot danger. An arctic hare's preferred food is arctic willow. However, it will also make do with lichens, moss, and other plants. A newborn arctic hare is actually brown in colour, turning white after 4 weeks.

Size: 43 to 70 centimetres; Weight: 6 to 15 lbs / 3 to 7 kg

Snow goose

Although snow geese are usually pure white in colour, many of them are darker grey, and called blue geese. In winter, they fly together in huge flocks to coastal marshes down south. They typically form a "V" shape when they fly. Have you noticed that? This formation is useful for reducing wind drag while they fly and also to avoid collision. A newly hatched snow goose has golden fuzz!

Size: 64 to 79 centimetres; Weight: 4.5 to 6 lbs / 2 to 3 kg

Arctic fox

An arctic fox is covered in thick fur, has a bushy tail, small ears and short muzzle – all of which help it to cope better with the bitter cold winters in the tundra. Arctic foxes have a keen sense of smell and can detect seal lairs up to a mile away. They create complex tunnels with over 100 entrances and extend for 150 metres.

Size: 70 to 110 centimetres; Weight: 6.6 to 17 lbs / 3 to 7.5 kg

Southern elephant seal

Southern elephant seals, the largest seal species, live in the sub-Antarctic and Antarctic waters. They have trunk-like inflatable snouts. A southern elephant seal can dive to an incredible depth of up to 1.4 kilometres underwater and hold its breath for up to 2 hours!

Size: 3.7 metres; Weight: 8,800 lbs / 3,990 kg

Ice worms

Ice worms are small worms found living in glaciers. They are related to earthworms and are the only type of worm that live all their lives in freezing cold glaciers. They make their way to the top of glaciers to feed on snow algae.

Size: 1 to 1.5 centimetres in length; Weight: 2 to 5 milligrams

Splendid Reptiles

Reptiles are cold-blooded animals with certain common features. They have rough, dry skin with scales, lay yolky eggs, breathe through lungs, shed their skin/scales periodically and give birth to young ones that are miniature versions of the adult.

Nile crocodile

Nile crocodiles are found in lakes and marshes around the Nile Basin, Africa and Madagascar. While most reptiles hatch eggs and move on, crocodiles are exceptionally caring parents, fiercely guarding eggs and helping the young ones hatch. Even though they feed mainly on fish, they also occasionally grab zebras, young hippos and deer near river banks.

Size: 4.1 to 5.2 metres; Weight: 500 to 1,650 lbs / 225 to 750 kg

Chameleon

Chameleons range in size from about a thumbnail to a domestic cat. The most special feature of a chameleon is its ability to change its skin colour to blend with the surroundings. It also has eyes that are capable of looking in two different directions independently. A chameleon also has a long, sticky tongue that can quickly grab insects at lightning speed!

Size: 2.8 to 68.5 centimetres; Weight: 0.02 to 4.4 lbs / 0.01 to 2 kg

Burmese python

A python can grow really large, with a girth as thick as a telephone pole! Young pythons spend most of their lives in trees. It is only when their size and weight doesn't allow them to climb or live comfortably in trees that they start living on the ground. They kill prey by suffocation: coiling their powerful body around the animal. "Baby" was a python holding the world record for the heaviest of its kind, weighing 400 pounds!

Size: 7 metres; Weight: 200 lbs / 90 kg

Prehensile-tailed skink

Prehensile-tailed skink is native to Solomon Islands and Papua New Guinea. Did you know that newborn skinks feed on the faeces of adults to develop useful gut bacteria needed for digestion? A social group of skinks is known as "circulus"!

Size: 76 centimetres; Weight: 0.8 to 1.75 lbs / 0.4 to 0.8 kg

Tuatara

Tuatara is a very unique reptile, found only in New Zealand. They are called "living fossils" because their closest relatives lived during the time of the dinosaurs. Apart from two regular eyes, they have an extra third eye on top of the head covered with scales and pigment and virtually invisible. This third eye helps the tuatara judge season and time of day.

Size: 80 centimetres;
Weight: 1.1 to 2.2 lbs / 0.5 to 1 kg

Diamondback terrapin

Diamondback terrapins get their name from diamond-shaped patterns on their shells. They live in salt marshes but need access to freshwater for rehydrating their bodies. In 2017, JFK airport in New York delayed its flights out for a special reason. The planes waited for dozens of female terrapins to cross the runways as they headed to the sandy perimeters to lay their eggs!

Size: 13 to 19 centimetres; Weight: 0.6 to 1.1 lbs / 0.25 to 0.5 kg

Leatherback turtle

A leatherback turtle gets its name from the type of shell on its back – instead of a hard shell, it has a soft, flexible and leathery shell. Leatherback turtles are better equipped for surviving cold waters than other turtle species due to a thick, insulating fat layer and a blood system that keeps the body warmer than the surroundings! Its favourite food is jellyfish.

Size: 1.8 to 2.2 metres; Weight: up to 2,000 lbs / 900 kg

They are the largest turtle species in the world

Galapagos giant tortoise

Galapagos giant tortoises are the longest living vertebrates on the planet, with an average lifespan of 100 years, some even living up to 150 years. They have slow metabolism and large water storage capacity – so they can go for up to a year without food or water!

Size: 1.3 metres; Weight: 919 lbs / 415 kg

Giant gecko

The New Caledonian giant gecko is one of the largest gecko species. They have brown, grey or yellowish green skin that helps them stay camouflaged among trees and vegetation. They generally live in trees, with the males on the lower branches guarding their territory while females dwell on the higher branches.

Size: 40 centimetres; Weight: 1.5 lbs / 0.7 kg

Amazing Amphibians

Amphibians are vertebrates that are adapted to live both in water and land, though some species live almost exclusively underwater. All amphibians, even those that thrive on land, need a moist environment. They can breathe through their skin and lay their eggs in water.

Chinese giant salamander

Chinese giant salamanders are the largest amphibians in the world. Even though they live underwater, they do not have gills. Instead, they absorb oxygen directly through their skin. So, they are usually found only in rivers, where oxygen is abundant. Did you know that a Chinese giant salamander is also known as baby fish? That's because they can make sounds like a baby crying.

Size: 1.2 – 1.8 metres;
Weight: 55 to 110 lbs / 25 to 50 kg

To detect their prey they sense the vibrations in the water

Mexican axolotl

A Mexican axolotl, and all axolotls, retain all their larval features throughout their lives. This means, an axolotl will keep its tadpole stage dorsal fin always. Very rarely, an axolotl might mature into an adult and live on land. Mexican axolotls are found exclusively in the Xochimilco Lake complex.

Size: 30 centimetres;
Weight: 0.6 lbs / 270 grams

Cane toad

Cane toads are poisonous amphibians that can grow really large and are active in the night. The heaviest known cane toad weighed 5 pounds! While many animals are affected by the venom, other predators are immune to it. Did you know that a cane toad's venom was used for coating arrow tips used by aboriginal hunters? Male cane toads are slightly smaller and have a more warty skin than the females.

Size: 10 to 24 centimetres;
Weight: 2.9 lbs / 1.3 kg

Surinam toad

A Surinam toad has a flat body, triangular head and tiny eyes. In fact, it looks very different from regular toads. Surinam toads give birth to young ones in the strangest possible way! Baby toads erupt out from tiny holes on the mother toad's back. They don't have to go through larval or tadpole stage. Unlike most toads that sit on their front legs, a Surinam toad lies down flat.

Size: 20 centimetres;
Weight: 3.5 to 5.6 lbs / 1.5 to 2.5 kg

Hellbender

The hellbender has another unique name: snot otter! This is because a hellbender secretes mucus through its skin when it is threatened. It is very similar to a mudpuppy but lacks the collar of external gills. Even though hellbenders have gills, they breathe almost exclusively through their skin.

Size: 30 to 74 centimetres; *Weight:* 3.3 to 5.5 lbs / 1.5 to 2.5 kg

Mudpuppy

Mudpuppies are also called waterdogs. A mudpuppy is among the few salamanders that can actually make sounds. Mudpuppies are usually found in lakes, ponds, streams and rivers, hiding under vegetation or logs. The most characteristic feature of a mudpuppy is its bushy, crimson external gills! The warmer and murkier its home, the longer its gills are.

Size: 33 centimetres;
Weight: 0.5 lbs / 225 grams

Caecilian

Caecilians are blind amphibians with no legs. They look like a cross between earthworms and snakes. Their tiny eyes can only detect the difference between light and dark. Even though they have no limbs, caecilians use their powerful skull and muscles to dig into dirt. A caecilian's skin is so smooth and slimy that it's almost impossible to catch hold of this slippery creature with your hands!

Size: 90 millimetres to 2.4 metres; *Weight:* up to 2.2 lbs / 1 kg

Red-eyed tree frog

The red-eyed tree frog is an iconic specimen of the Amazon rainforest. Its bright body and eye colouration is an important adaptation for scaring predators. This frog species is not venomous, though. It has an extra eyelid over the eye to act as a transparent veil, which still allows the frog to see well. Did you know that the eggs of a red-eyed tree frog hatch within seconds when attacked?

Size: 3 to 7 centimetres;
Weight: 0.01 to 0.03 lbs / 5 to 15 grams

California newt

The Californian newt is a medium-sized salamander with rough, grainy skin. It varies in colour from yellowish brown to deep brown. All adult California newts are toxic and their skin secretes a type of neurotoxin called tetrodoxin, similar to what is secreted by puffer fish.

Size: 12.5 to 20 centimetres; *Weight:* 0.01 to 0.02 lbs / 5 to 10 grams

Magnificent Mammals

Mammals are vertebrates that give birth to young ones and feed them milk. All mammals have fur or hair, well-developed brains and three tiny bones in their middle ear!

Flying squirrel

A flying squirrel, despite its name, cannot fly. Instead, it glides for 45 to 150 metres in the air using its furry membrane called "patagium". This flap of loose skin acts just like a hang glider. The woolly flying squirrel is the largest species, while Hose's pygmy flying squirrel is the smallest.

*Size: up to 60 centimetres;
Weight: 3.5 ounces to 5.5 lbs / 100 grams to 2.5 kg*

While gliding, they can turn and change their angle of descent

Aardvark

Aardvarks are commonly found in Africa and their name means "earth pig". They have a snout like a pig, a tail like a kangaroo and ears like a rabbit, but they are not related to any of these animals. These "antbears" forage in grasslands and forests and use their long, worm-like tongue to find and slurp up insects. Their favourite food is termites, eaten straight from a mound!

Size: 1 to 1.3 metres; Weight: 110 to 180 lbs / 50 to 80 kg

Wolf

A wolf is the largest member of the dog family. Its most characteristic feature is its howl. Wolves often howl to communicate with each other or send messages to other packs about their territory. Wolves hunt in small packs of 6 to 10 members. Even though wolves are carnivorous, they may occasionally feed on fruits. After humans and cattle, grey wolves are the most common mammals in the planet!

Size: 0.9 to 1.6 metres; Weight: 40 to 175 lbs / 18 to 80 kg

Zebra

There are three different species of this amazing striped mammal – the plains zebra, mountain zebra and Grevy's zebra. All of them are found in Africa. A zebra's prominent feature is its stripes – they might help zebras recognize each other, confuse predators or even regulate heat! Closely related to horses, zebras live in herds. Their fierce fighting skills help them team up to tackle predators.

*Size: 2.2 to 2.5 metres;
Weight: 440 to 1,000 lbs / 200 to 450 kg*

Yak

Yaks are high-altitude dwelling cousins of cows with shaggy fur covering their body and curved horns. They have three times the lung capacity of regular cows to survive in the mountainous regions where oxygen is low. Yaks were domesticated to carry loads about 5,000 years ago.

*Size: 2.5 to 3.3 metres;
Weight: 770 to 1290 lbs / 350 to 585 kg*

Naked mole rat

A naked mole rat is a rodent just like a mouse or the common brown rat, but there is one major difference – it does not have fur like the other members. Additionally it also has a wrinkly body and long front teeth that makes it look like a miniature walrus. These rodents live in colonies with one dominant queen rat, much like bees or ants!

Size: 20 to 33 centimetres;
Weight: 3.3 lbs / 1.5kg

Giant pangolin

The giant pangolin is the largest pangolin species and has a body covered in tough scales, making it look like a giant, walking pinecone. When a pangolin encounters a predator, it quickly rolls itself into a ball. Additionally, it can also give out an unpleasant smell that drives many animals away. They feed on insects, especially termites and ants.

Size 1.2 to 1.4 metres;
Weight: up to 70 lbs / 32 kg

Bat

Despite the bad rap bats have received as fanged, spooky creatures, they are far from dangerous and actually useful to humans! Bats feed on millions of pests thus saving crops. Nectar-feeding bats help in pollination and fruit bats help disperse seeds. A bat is the only mammal capable of flight. It roosts by hanging upside down! Vampire bats are the only species that feed on blood – though only that of cattle and wild beasts!

Size: 2 to 30 centimetres;
Weight: 0.7 ounces to 3.3 lbs / 20 grams to 1.5 kg

Horse

Horses are familiar domesticated animals though there are several wild horse species, too. In the wild, they gather in groups ranging from 3 to 20, led by a stallion (older male) with mares (female horses) and foals (young horses) in the group. Interestingly, when a foal turns into a colt (when they turn two years old), the stallion drives them out of the group! Since horses don't have an efficient digestive system, they need to eat constantly. Racehorses can run at speeds of 67 kilometres per hour.

Size: 1.7 metres;
Weight: up to 2,200 lbs / 1,000 kg

Hippopotamus

Hippos are heavy, semi-aquatic mammals with barrel-shaped bodies, and are the largest animals on land after the elephant. They often wallow in ponds or swamps to cool down on hot days. Despite their bulky bodies, hippos are excellent swimmers! A male hippo simply opens its mouth to display its curved teeth to scare away other males.

Size: 3.5 metres; Weight: up to 7,000 lbs / 3,175 kg

The Big Cats

The big cats include the most ferocious predators in grasslands, forests and mountains across the world. Of the different big cat species, the lion and the tiger are the largest. Their sharp teeth, strong jaws and powerful muscles make them formidable animals.

Asiatic tiger

Tigers are the biggest cats in the world. They hunt singly by stalking their prey silently and pouncing and delivering a bite in the neck. While most big cats avoid water, tigers enjoy cooling themselves in streams. Did you know that no two tigers have the same pattern of stripes – each tiger has a unique pattern!

Size: 3.3 metres; Weight: 800 lbs / 360 kg

Jaguar

Jaguars are the only big cats found in the Western hemisphere. Among the big cats, relative to their size, jaguars deliver the most powerful bite! Jaguars live in both rainforests and grasslands. A jaguar marks its territory by clawing trees. Many South American cultures and folklore worship jaguars as gods!

Size: 1.2 to 2 metres;
Weight: 100 to 250 lbs / 45 to 115 kg

Cougar

A cougar is known by many different names – puma, mountain lion and panther. They occasionally catch deer though they mostly feed on raccoons, porcupines and coyotes. They typically hide a carcass in a suitable spot and feed on it for many days. A cougar can spring over 5 metres up into the air from a sitting position.

Size: 1 to 1.5 metres;
Weight: 136 lbs / 62 kg

Leopard

Leopards are found in Asia and Africa. A leopard is so comfortable climbing trees that it can even haul its prey up there to eat! It does that to keep the flesh safe from scavengers like hyenas and foxes. The spots on its fur helps it blend well with the tree branches and shadows and it might often leap down to catch an animal.

Size: 0.7 metres; Weight: 66 to 176 lbs / 30 to 80 kg

Bobcat

Bobcats are wild cats about twice as big as domestic cats. They have long legs and tufted ears like lynxes. The bobcat gets its name for its stumpy tail, which appears to be "bobbed" or cut at the end. Even though they usually catch fish and small animals, these fierce hunters can sometimes catch larger prey, too.

Size: 69 centimetres;
Weight: 14 to 40 lbs / 6 to 18 kg

Cheetah

The cheetah has the distinction of being the fastest terrestrial mammal! It can easily go from 0 to 96 kilometres per hour in just 3 seconds. While chasing its prey, it can also quickly change direction if needed. As you can guess, such a chase can cost a cheetah lots of energy, so it scans the area first before setting off. Did you know that a cheetah is the only big cat that doesn't roar?

Size: 1.1 to 1.5 metres;
Weight: 77 to 143 lbs / 35 to 65 kg

Clouded leopard

Clouded leopards are found in Asia, ranging from the rainforests in Indonesia to the foothills of the Himalayas. Though all the big cats are great climbers, the clouded leopard has quite extraordinary climbing skills. It has short, powerful legs with rotating ankles, useful for climbing down trees like a squirrel.

Size: 0.6 to 0.9 metres;
Weight: up to 50 lbs / 23 kg

Snow leopard

Snow leopards live in the cold mountainous regions of Asia and Siberia, and have thick fur to keep themselves warm. Their feet are wide and covered in fur, acting like snowshoes, helping them navigate across the snow easily. They have powerful legs and can jump about 15 metres in a leap!

Size: 1.2 to 1.5 metres;
Weight: 60 to 120 lbs / 27 to 54 kg

Lion

Lions are the most social creatures among big cats and live in groups called "prides". Male lions defend the territory while the females hunt and bring food. Despite being referred to as the "king of the jungle", lions mostly lives in grasslands. They have powerful claws and strong muscles to overpower their prey and sharp teeth. Only male lions have manes. The darker the mane, the older the lion!

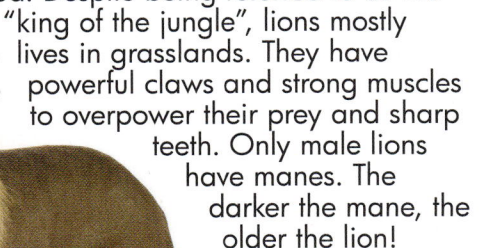

Size: 1.3 to 2 metres;
Weight: 265 to 420 lbs / 120 to 190 kg

Black panther

A black panther is usually a black-coloured jaguar or leopard. They have plain black coats or black spots against a dark fur. The difference in colouration is due to levels of melanin pigments. Black panthers are rarely seen. They have excellent camouflage while hunting in the dark.

Size: 2.4 metres;
Weight: 115 to 220 lbs / 52 to 100 kg

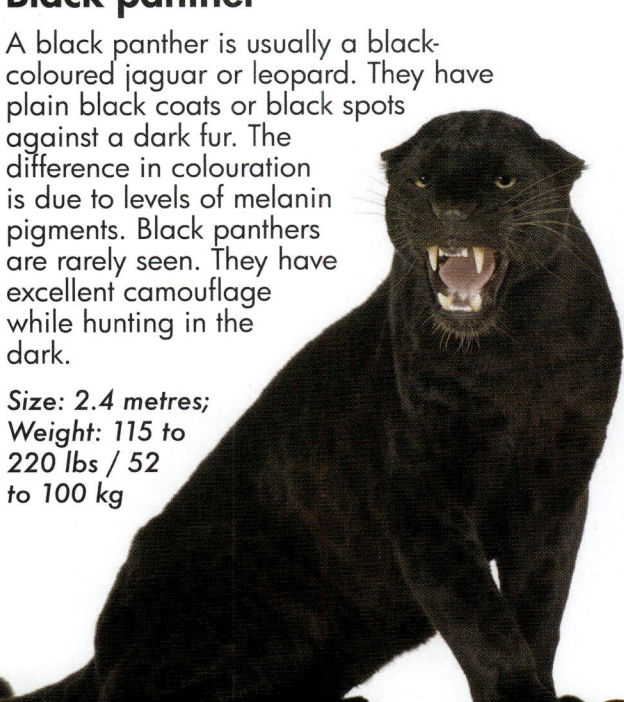

Mighty Bears

Bears are heavily built, bulky mammals with short tails, shaggy fur and powerful jaws, strong paws and broad skulls. Most bear species are excellent climbers. They have an excellent sense of smell and are omnivores by nature – that is, they eat almost anything!

Sun bear

A sun bear is the smallest and rarest among the bear species. It has a distinct yellow patch on its chest not found in the other bears. Sun bears are excellent climbers. They are found in Southeast Asian rainforests.

Size: 1.2 to 1.5 metres;
Weight: 60 to 150 lbs / 27 to 68 kg

Spectacled bear

Spectacled bear is the only bear species native to South America, found in the dense jungles of the Andes. They have red, brown or black fur and sometimes have yellowish rings around their eyes that give them the name "spectacled bear". They live at high altitudes and descend only to look for food.

Size: 1.8 metres; Weight: 220 to 340 lbs / 100 to 155 kg

Polar bear

All animals living in the cold tundra regions have certain adaptations – and polar bears have them too. The thick fur and blubber layers protect them while out in the cold or swimming in freezing waters! Did you know that polar bears have black skin under their fur? They wait near seal breathing holes to grab their prey as they're not quick enough to chase them in the water!

Size: 1.8 to 3 metres; Weight: 770 to 1,500 lbs / 350 to 680 kg

American black bear

The American black bears live in Mexico, the United States and Canada. Its coat consists of several layers of shaggy fur that help the bear stay warm during the winter season. A black bear is an expert tree climber despite being bulky and heavy! Sometimes, it stands on its hind legs to sniff scents.

Size: 1.4 metres;
Weight: 660 lbs / 300 kg

Sloth bear

Sloth bears are native to Asia and have brownish to black fur with a characteristic pattern on their chest. They typically feed on ants and termites and use their long, curved claws to break ant mounds and suck in the insects. They also feed on flowers or fruits. They can stand on their hind legs to threaten a predator. A sloth bear is the only bear species that carries its young ones on its back!

Size: 1.5 to 2 metres; Weight: 200 to 300 lbs / 90 to 135 kg

Brown bear

Brown bears are found in Asia, Europe and North America and some of the largest brown bears are found in British Columbia, Alaska and Kodiak Island. Even though these bears are mostly solitary, they sometimes gather in large groups, especially in fishing spots where salmon swim upstream. They can eat 9 pounds of food in a day, often storing enough fat to make it through winter.

Size: 1.4 to 2.8 metres long; Weight: 700 lbs / 315 kg

Asiatic black bear

Asiatic black bears have dark fur with a white patch on the chest in the shape of "V". They are found in forests, hills and mountains. They have strong, broad paws with curved claws that are ideal for climbing trees and digging for food. Since they are particularly fond of fruits, they climb and even wait on trees for the fruits to ripen!

Size: 1.2 to 1.9 metres;
Weight: 198 to 254 lbs / 90 to 115 kg

Primates

Primates are mammals that have large brains in comparison to their body size. Humans come under this category, too! They are also good at climbing, with special toes and arms for grasping on to support. Primates are good at judging distances and can use various tools.

Chimpanzee

Chimpanzees are closely related to us and are very social by nature. They can walk on all fours (also called knuckle-walking) and also walk upright. They can swing across tree branches efficiently. Grooming each other is an important part of their lives, and they look for lice, ticks and dirt on each other's bodies. Chimps have been known to use sticks as tools to look for food.

Size: 1 to 1.7 metres (standing); Weight: 70 to 130 lbs / 32 to 68 kg

Baboon

Of the five different baboon species known, all of them live in Africa or Arabia. They prefer the savannah and semi-arid habitats though they also live in tropical forests. Baboons have been known to use different sounds to communicate with each other. In Africa, they often raid crops and are considered as pests!

Size: 0.4 to 0.5 metres; Weight: 33 to 82 lbs / 15 to 37 kg

Spider monkey

Spider monkeys are found in the tropical rainforests in South and Central America and Mexico. They live in large groups and sleep together in smaller groups. They feed on a variety of fruits, seeds and nuts and even bird eggs and spiders! They are very noisy and often screech, bark or make other sounds.

Size: 35 to 66 centimetres; Weight: 13 lbs / 6 kg

Gorilla

Although gorillas have been shown as aggressive, chest-beating, monstrous creatures, they are actually gentle and peaceful animals. They display emotions like humans and are our closest cousins after chimps and bonobos. They are the largest among primates and often build nests in trees or on the ground.

Size: 1.6 metres; Weight: up to 440 lbs / 200 kg

Bush baby

Bush babies, also called "galagos" and "nagapies", have unique, saucer-shaped large eyes. They mostly live in trees and are active in the night. They are excellent jumpers and can spring across quickly to snatch insects or escape from predators!

Size: 38 to 40 centimetres; Weight: 13.25 lbs / 6 kg

Tamarin

Tamarins and marmosets are closely related. Golden lion tamarin is the most spectacular species of tamarin and has an impressive golden mane much like lions. Both the male and female tamarins are good parents, often carrying around their young ones on their backs.

Size: 13 to 30 centimetres; Weight: 0.5 to 2 lbs / 0.25 to 1 kg

Gray langur

Gray langur, also called Hanuman monkey, is native to the Indian subcontinent, found from the Himalayan Mountains to Sri Lanka. They have a black face but grey fur covering their body. They are primarily herbivores and will not only eat fruits and flowers but also pine cones, spider webs, moss and lichens!

Size: 60 centimetres; Weight: 28 lbs / 12.5 kg

Capuchin

Capuchins are small monkeys with white, cream or light tan fur on their faces and dark brown coats and communicate with each other through different types of calls. They live on trees and come down only in search of water.

Size: 34 to 45 centimetres; Weight: 3 to 9 lbs / 1.5 to 4 kg

Marmoset

Marmosets are small monkeys with soft and silky fur and tufts of hair on their faces. They come in a variety of colours ranging from brown and black to silver and even bright orange! A marmoset cannot use its tail to catch hold of a branch, but it is useful for balance.

Size: 48 centimetres; Weight: 0.5 lbs / 225 grams

Ocean Dwellers - Sharks

Sharks are a type of fish called elasmobranchii and have skeletons not made of bone but of a type of tough tissue called cartilage. While most fish only have one pair of gills, sharks usually have five to seven pairs. True to reputation, many shark species can detect a drop of blood from a mile away, thanks to their amazing senses.

Hammerhead shark

A hammerhead shark's head is oddly shaped, but the eyes positioned on either ends of its head help improve its vision for hunting. They can see above and below all the time! They feed on a variety of fish, octopuses, squids, and their favourite food – stingrays. They can use their broad heads to pin down stingrays to the seafloor to trap them. While many hammerhead sharks are small, the great hammerhead shark is large, measuring 6 metres and weighing 1,000 pounds.

Size: 4 to 6 metres; Weight: 500 to 1,000 lbs / 225 to 450 kg

Thresher shark

A thresher shark's most recognizable feature is its long caudal fin that is nearly half of its total body length. Thresher sharks have small, curved and razor-sharp teeth and vary in colour from blue to metallic brown.

Size: 6.1 metres; Weight: 1,100 lbs / 500 kg

Cookiecutter shark

A cookiecutter shark has a long and thin body and a cone-shaped snout. It has the largest teeth in proportion to its body. It gets its name from the cut it leaves when it bites. Did you know that cookiecutter sharks swallow the teeth they shed? This helps to strengthen their skeleton, actually. Even though they swim closer to the surface to hunt for food, they often dwell at depths of 90 metres under the surface.

Size: 50 centimetres

Bull shark

Bull sharks are aggressive and powerful sharks found near shores of tropical areas and can even venture into freshwater bodies. Bull sharks, along with tiger sharks and great white sharks, are among the most dangerous sharks in the world. A bull shark has a flat, blunt nose, grey on the top and white underneath. They have a habit of head-butting a prey before launching an attack.

Size: 3.3 metres; *Weight:* 200 to 500 lbs / 90 to 225 kg

Great white shark

The movie *Jaws* was inspired by the great white shark, and though it is a dangerous species, it is not as fearsome as mindlessly attacking people. But they are still the largest predatory sharks in the world! They have streamlined, torpedo-shaped bodies and powerful tails to propel themselves forward. With 300 serrated, triangular teeth, in many rows, they are formidable predators!

Size: 3.4 to 6.4 metres;
Weight: 4,200 to 5,000 lbs / 1,900 to 2,250 kg

Shortfin mako shark

Shortfin mako sharks are migratory, travelling long distances every year. They feed on a variety of fish, turtles, squids and other smaller sharks. They are found in tropical and temperate oceans across the world.

Size: 3.8 metres; *Weight:* 1,200 lbs / 540 kg

Tasselled wobbegong

The tasselled wobbegong is a type of shark with a flat body, colouration and markings on its body and branched skin flaps to camouflage effectively amidst coral reefs. In fact, it sits motionless on the seafloor and grabs at an unsuspecting prey passing by that way.

Size: 1.25 to 3.2 metres;
Weight: 154 lbs / 70 kg

Goblin shark

A goblin shark is a rare, strange-looking shark that dwells in the deep sea. It has a pink body and a strangely shaped head. It is rarely seen and mostly thrives on a diet of fish, crabs and other molluscs. It spends most of its life in darkness in the ocean depths and hence has poor eyesight. Its teeth are visible even with its mouth closed!

Size: 1.75 metres; *Weight:* 460 lbs / 210 kg

Ocean Dwellers - Cetaceans

Whales, dolphins and porpoises are classified under the group called cetaceans. They are aquatic mammals that are large and mostly inhabit oceans, with only a few living in freshwater. They are not only intelligent, but also social creatures.

Harbour porpoise

Harbour porpoises are found in shallow waters along coasts. These shy creatures are among the smallest cetacean species. Instead of a snout like dolphins, they have blunt noses, black lips that curve inwards and spade-shaped teeth. Since they are elusive and avoid attention, they are very rarely spotted.

Size: 1.4 to 1.9 metres;
Weight: 168 lbs / 76 kg

Narwhal

With its fascinating horn, a narwhal is the unicorn of the oceans! A type of porpoise, it is often seen along the coasts of the Arctic ocean. A narwhal has two teeth and in male narwhals, one tooth grows into a long, sword-like spiral tusk. Narwhals often travel and hunt in groups, sometimes numbering hundreds or even thousands!

Size: 5.1 metres; Weight: 1,760 to 3,530 lbs / 800 to 1,600 kg

Blue whale

The blue whale is huge – the largest blue whale ever known measured 33 metres. Its tongue alone measures as much as an elephant. It is the largest creature on the planet. Did you know that a blue whale can be really loud? As the loudest animal on Earth, a blue whale can produce sounds as high as 188 decibels. For comparison, a jet engine produces a sound of 140 decibels. It has to feed on 8,000 pounds of food every day.

Size: 25 to 30 metres; Weight: Up to 380,000 lbs / 172 tonnes

Bottlenose dolphin

Bottlenose dolphins are friendly, social creatures that often squeak and squawk to communicate with each other. They can jump up to 6 metres high from the water. Dolphins have an excellent sense of hearing. Did you know that bottlenose dolphins shed their outermost layer of skin every two hours?

Size: 2.5 to 3.5 metres;
Weight: 440 to 1,100 lbs / 200 to 500 kg

Killer whale (Orca)

Also known as orca, the killer whale is the largest species in the dolphin family. They have a distinct black and white body colouration and are found in all the oceans in the world. They often hunt together, much like a pack of wolves! They are carnivores and primarily hunt for seals.

Size: 5 to 8 metres; Weight: 12,000 lbs / 5,450 kg

Beluga whale

The beluga whale, also called white whale, is among the smallest whale species. The young calves are born grey or brown but fade into a white colour as they become adults. They do not have dorsal fins and have prominent rounded foreheads. Beluga whales live together in small groups, called "pods". They communicate through whistles, clicks and clangs and can also imitate other sounds! Did you know that the vertebrae in the beluga's neck are not fused, giving the species greater mobility and flexibility in its neck!

Size: 4 to 76 metres; Weight: 2,000 to 3,000 lbs / 900 to 1,350 kg

Manatee

Manatees, also called sea cows, are closely related to dugongs but lack the distinct forked tails of dugongs. Despite its bulky body, a manatee is an excellent swimmer, and usually glides or swims underwater in search of food. Manatees have voracious appetites and often graze for 8 hours a day. Calves are born underwater and taken to the surface for their first breath by their mother!

Size: 2.8 to 3.5 metres; Weight: 880 to 1,200 lbs / 400 to 545 kg

Dugong

Dugongs are large sea mammals that are related to an elephant but don't look very similar. They are vegetarians, grazing on grasses underwater. They can hold their breath for about 6 minutes and have to resurface frequently. Sometimes, they stand on their tails, with their head above the surface. They have a forked tail like that of a whale, and it's possible that dugongs might have been the inspiration for old-time folktales about mermaids.

Size: 2.6 metres; Weight: 590 to 920 lbs / 270 to 415 kg

Humpback whale

Humpback whales are named for the small hump found in front of the dorsal fins. They are found in oceans all over the world. Humpback whales are most well-known for their long and fascinating "whale songs". Even calves have been observed whispering to their mothers. Whale songs are very likely a form of communication and way for finding mates.

Size: 15 to 16 metres; Weight: 72,000 lbs / 32 tonnes

Extinct Animals

When any species is completely eliminated from the wild, and unable to reproduce and have offspring, this is known as extinction. During millions of years, many animal species on earth have faced extinction. Some species become extinct due to climate change but in more recent times many species have been wiped out due to loss of their natural habitats and from human activities.

Woolly mammoth

Woolly mammoths were about the same size as our present day elephants and were closely related to Asian elephants. Unlike elephants, they had thick fur covering their body. They had long, curved tusks that were probably useful for fighting and defence. They became extinct about 10,000 years ago at the end of the last (and most recent) Ice Age.

Size: 4 metres; Weight: 12,000 lbs / 5,400 kg

Sabre-toothed tiger

Sabre-toothed tigers were a ferocious predator that had curved canine teeth that might have been useful for holding on to prey. They are estimated to have gone extinct around 10,000 years ago. Possibly, climate change, decline in the population of their prey and human activity could have caused the extinction of this fascinating tiger species.

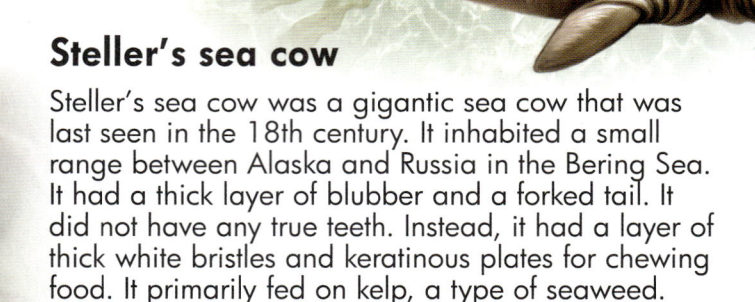

Size: 1.1 metres; Weight: 880 lbs / 400 kg

Steller's sea cow

Steller's sea cow was a gigantic sea cow that was last seen in the 18th century. It inhabited a small range between Alaska and Russia in the Bering Sea. It had a thick layer of blubber and a forked tail. It did not have any true teeth. Instead, it had a layer of thick white bristles and keratinous plates for chewing food. It primarily fed on kelp, a type of seaweed.

Size: 7.6 metres; Weight: 17,600 lbs / 8,000 kg

Quagga

The quagga was a zebra species that was found widely in South Africa. After the European settlers started hunting them they were completely exterminated in the wild. The last quagga died in a zoo in Amsterdam in 1883. Unlike the zebra, which had black stripes on a white body, quagga had a body similar to a horse and stripes only on the front part.

Size: 1.2 to 1.4 metres; Weight: 550 to 660 lbs / 250 to 300 kg

Thylacine

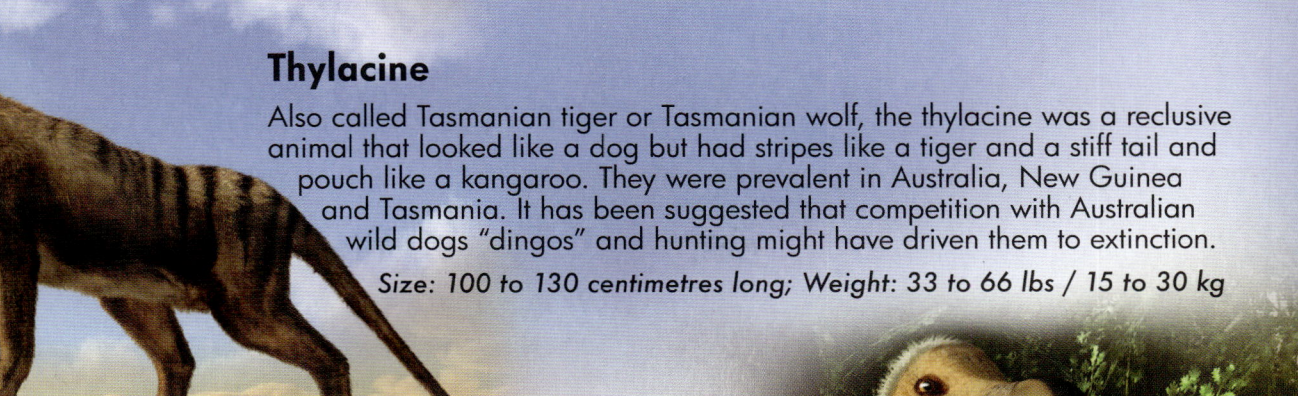

Also called Tasmanian tiger or Tasmanian wolf, the thylacine was a reclusive animal that looked like a dog but had stripes like a tiger and a stiff tail and pouch like a kangaroo. They were prevalent in Australia, New Guinea and Tasmania. It has been suggested that competition with Australian wild dogs "dingos" and hunting might have driven them to extinction.

Size: 100 to 130 centimetres long; Weight: 33 to 66 lbs / 15 to 30 kg

Dodo

The Dodo was a flightless bird that was found in Mauritius in the Indian Ocean. Famously mentioned in *Alice in Wonderland*, these birds were discovered by Portuguese sailors and were driven to extinction by hunting as well through the introduction of rodents that fed on their eggs. The dodo was a large, flightless bird, bigger than a turkey, with small wings.

Size: 1 metre; Weight: Up to 39 lbs / 17.5 kg

Great auk

Great auks were large flightless birds that bred in colonies in the rocky islands along the North Atlantic coasts. Despite their resemblance to penguins, due to the fact they stood erect with a black and white body, they are not closely related. Without any means of defence or way to escape, these birds were mostly hunted to extinction.

Size: 30 to 50 centimetres; Weight: 11 lbs / 5 kg

Auroch

Aurochs were large sized wild oxen that once inhabited Europe. At least two species of aurochs were domesticated by early humans. They were one of the largest herbivores in Europe after the Ice Age. They had massive curved horns and considered the ancestors of the modern-day cattle. The last known live auroch died in 1627.

Size: 1.8 metres; Weight: 1,500 lbs / 680 kg

Southern gastric brooding frog

The Southern Gastric brooding frog was a rare frog species that was mostly aquatic and found in creeks and rock pools. They have not been found in the wild since 1981. What's unique about this frog species was the reproduction. The mother frogs swallowed fertilized eggs and during the entire period did not eat anything. Once the tadpoles were fully developed, the mother expelled them out by explosive vomiting.

Size: 33 to 54 millimetres

Prehistoric Creatures (Marine)

The creatures that lived during prehistoric times were quite different from the animals we see today. They were much larger in size, possibly due to the higher levels of oxygen millions of years ago.

Basilosaurus

This gigantic, fierce creature whose name means "king lizard" was not a lizard; it was type of shark that could grow to 20 metres. It was probably the largest carnivore of its time, and went extinct millions of years ago due to climate change. It had rows of oversized, pointed, conical teeth ideal for nabbing a variety of sharks and smaller whales for food!

Size: 21 metres; Weight: 132,000 lbs / 60 tonnes

Megalodon

Megalodon was the largest ever shark species and one of the biggest fish to have ever lived in the oceans. It thrived for 13 million years, before going extinct. It lived in warm tropical and subtropical waters and was a fierce and dominant predator. All the fossils recovered from the megalodon sharks are teeth. How did this mega shark species go extinct? It's believed to have become extinct along with other animal species around the time when global cooling occurred.

Size: 14 to 16 metres; Weight: 120,000 lbs / 55 tonnes

Liopleurodon

Liopleurodon was a top predator that thrived in the oceans during the Jurassic era. This gigantic beast often preyed on other smaller marine animals. It had a specialised nose designed to smell underwater. Even though they weren't as swift as the great white sharks of today, they were certainly efficient at propelling themselves forward with their long flippers.

Size: 5 to 7 metres; Weight: 300,000 lbs / 136 tonnes

Giant ammonite

This predatory squid-like creature also had a protective, coil-shaped shell like a snail. Even though it continuously grew its shell, it only lived in the outer chamber. With beak-like jaws and a ring of tentacles, the giant ammonites preyed on other smaller fish and marine creatures. These giant ammonites would have been larger than an average human being!

Size: up to 2.7 metres; Weight: 3,300 lbs / 1,500 kg

Ancient sea scorpion (Jaekelopterus)

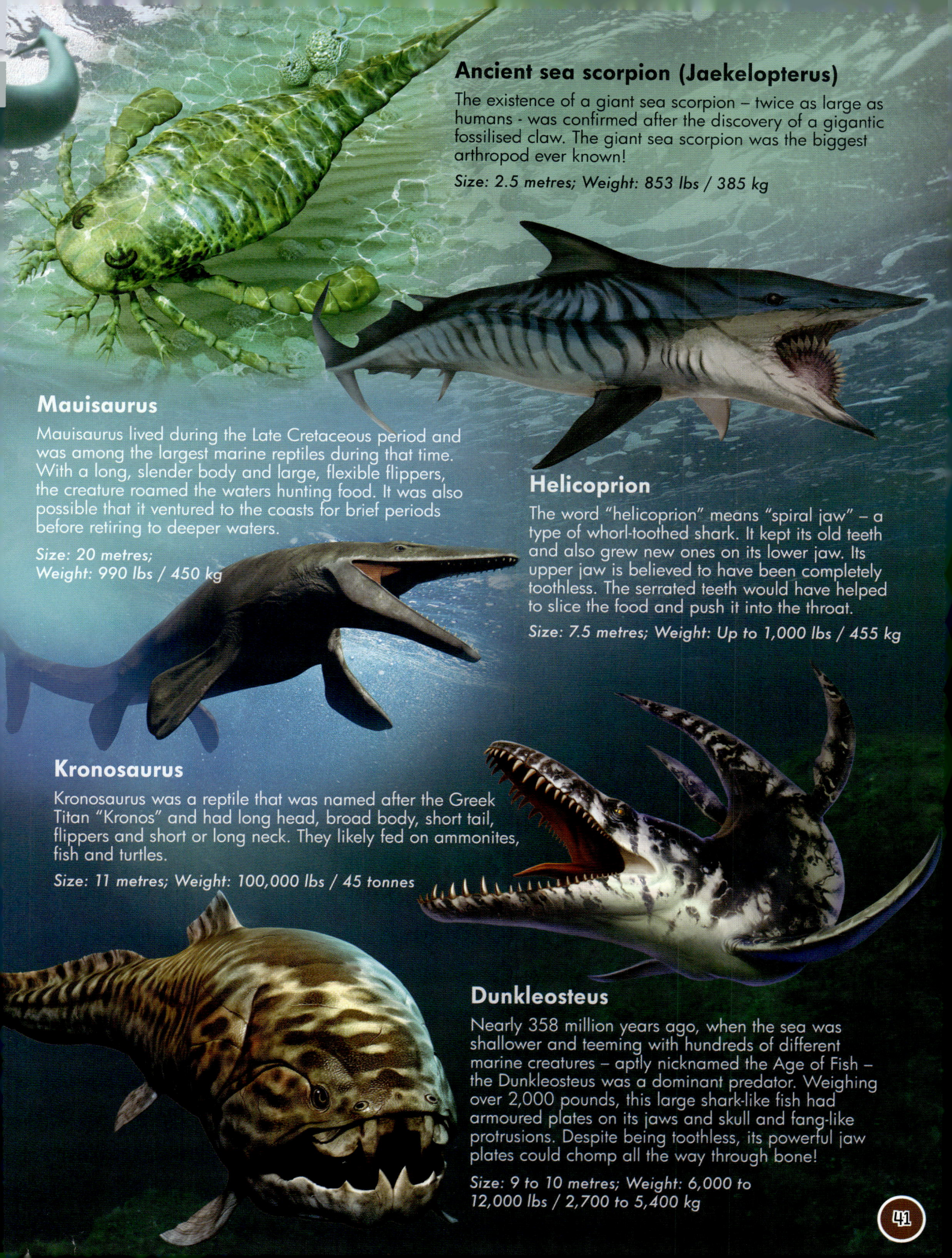

The existence of a giant sea scorpion – twice as large as humans - was confirmed after the discovery of a gigantic fossilised claw. The giant sea scorpion was the biggest arthropod ever known!

Size: 2.5 metres; Weight: 853 lbs / 385 kg

Mauisaurus

Mauisaurus lived during the Late Cretaceous period and was among the largest marine reptiles during that time. With a long, slender body and large, flexible flippers, the creature roamed the waters hunting food. It was also possible that it ventured to the coasts for brief periods before retiring to deeper waters.

*Size: 20 metres;
Weight: 990 lbs / 450 kg*

Helicoprion

The word "helicoprion" means "spiral jaw" – a type of whorl-toothed shark. It kept its old teeth and also grew new ones on its lower jaw. Its upper jaw is believed to have been completely toothless. The serrated teeth would have helped to slice the food and push it into the throat.

Size: 7.5 metres; Weight: Up to 1,000 lbs / 455 kg

Kronosaurus

Kronosaurus was a reptile that was named after the Greek Titan "Kronos" and had long head, broad body, short tail, flippers and short or long neck. They likely fed on ammonites, fish and turtles.

Size: 11 metres; Weight: 100,000 lbs / 45 tonnes

Dunkleosteus

Nearly 358 million years ago, when the sea was shallower and teeming with hundreds of different marine creatures – aptly nicknamed the Age of Fish – the Dunkleosteus was a dominant predator. Weighing over 2,000 pounds, this large shark-like fish had armoured plates on its jaws and skull and fang-like protrusions. Despite being toothless, its powerful jaw plates could chomp all the way through bone!

Size: 9 to 10 metres; Weight: 6,000 to 12,000 lbs / 2,700 to 5,400 kg

Prehistoric Creatures (Terrestrial)

Dinosaurs are undoubtedly the most well-known prehistoric creatures, thanks to movies and extensive research. However, several other fascinating reptiles and mammals inhabited the lands during the Earth's history, ranging from gigantic plant-eating sloths to tiny shrew-like creatures.

Megazostrodon

This small rodent-like creature lived around 200 or 250 million years ago. It was active in the night and probably fed on insects. Even though it had a few mammal-like features, it also had other reptilian characteristics. Resembling a shrew, a megazostrodon probably burrowed or climbed trees just like the rats of today.

Size: 10 to 12 centimetres; Weight: 0.04 to 0.06 lbs / 18 to 30 grams

Megatherium

The sloths of today are small, but Megatherium was a gigantic ground sloth that was at least 10 times as big as the present-day ones. Standing on its hind legs, it would have been a whopping 3.5 metres tall. Despite having big claws and large teeth, these herbivores only fed on leaves and vegetation.

Size: 6 metres; Weight: 8,800 lbs / 4,000 kg

Repenomamus

Repenomamus was a large mammal that lived at the same time as dinosaurs and probably feasted on them. This badger-like creature measured about 1 metre, much smaller than many gigantic dinosaurs, but larger than a few ground and flying species they fed on.

Size: 1 metre; Weight: 26 to 31 lbs / 12 to 14 kg

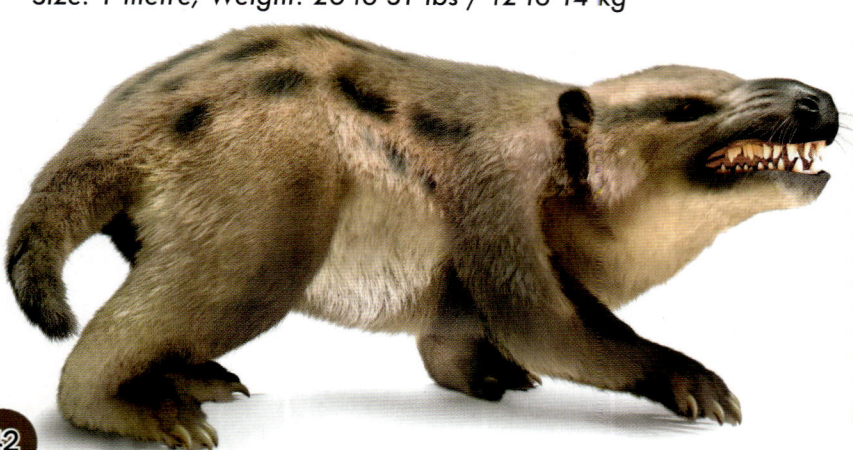

Indricotherium

Related to the rhino of today but without the horn (and with a longer neck) Indricotherium was the largest mammal of its time. It also weighed up to 60,000 pounds – that's about four times as much as an elephant! This herbivore lived in the forests of central Asia around 23 to 34 million years ago.

Size: 5 metres; Weight: 40,000 – 60,000 lbs / 18 to 27 tonnes

Quetzalcoatlus

Quetzalcoatlus was one of the largest flying reptiles ever known! This toothless creature was as tall as a giraffe and had the wingspan of an F-16 fighter plane. Despite its giant size and stiff neck, it glided well through the sky. It also had a crest on its head and a sharp beak like that of a stork. It probably fed on small dinosaurs or leftover carcasses.

Size: 10 to 11 metres; Weight: 440 to 550 lbs / 200 to 250 kg

Glyptodon

Glyptodon was a gigantic mammal with a prominent armour covering its body – very similar to armadillos and tortoises. Even its tail was armoured but separated from the shell covering the rest of the body. A fully grown Glyptodon could be the size of a car and very possibly hunted by humans for the bony shells that might have been used as temporary shelters during bad weather.

Size: 3.3 metres; Weight: 4,400 lbs / 2,000 kg

Elasmotherium

Often referred to as the Siberian unicorn, this creature was actually an ancient rhino species covered in fur that could have possibly been around at the same time as humans. Elasmotherium lived on the grasslands of Russia, Ukraine, Kazakhstan and Siberia. Did you know that this creature weighed twice as much as the rhinoceros of today?

Size: 5 metres; Weight: 7,200 to 9,000 lbs / 3,250 to 4,000 kg

Titanoboa

If you thought an anaconda was scary big, then you should hear about the titanoboa that grew to about 12 metres and weighed nearly 2,500 pounds! The fossil of this gigantic snake was first discovered in a large coal mine in Colombia. Titanoboa, about 10 times as large as the anaconda, lived in the lush forests of South America, as well as the waters, and were good swimmers.

Size: 12 metres; Weight: 2,500 lbs / 1,150 kg

Prehistoric Creatures (Dinosaurs)

Dinosaurs were reptiles that dominated the planet for millions of years, during the Jurassic, Triassic and Cretaceous periods. We know about dinosaurs (terrible lizards), thanks to the several fossils discovered in different places in the world. These reptiles ranged from herbivores to carnivores of all sizes!

Brachiosaurus

Brachiosaurus was a huge dinosaur with a long neck and was much bigger than any land animals you can find today. Another unusual feature was that its forelegs were longer than its hind legs. These gigantic herbivores fed on coniferous trees, cycads and ginkgoes. These dinosaurs probably lived in herds and communicated by making hoots like a whale.

Size: 18 to 21 metres; Weight: 56,000 to 116,000 lbs / 25 to 52 tonnes

Triceratops

Triceratops was a herbivore with a large, impressive head with three horns (two big and one small) and a protective plate. It also had a bony frill at the back of its head. The horns came in very useful to defend itself when threatened by predators. It was about the size of an African elephant. The head of a Triceratops was one of the largest among land animals, making up nearly one-third of its body length!

Size: 9 metres; Weight: 11,000 lbs / 5 tonnes

Tyrannosaurus rex

Tyrannosaurus is easily one of the most popular dinosaurs ever discovered! True to its reputation, this "king of tyrant lizards" had a massive body, powerful jaws and sharp teeth and dominated the scene during its time, feeding on smaller dinosaurs and sometimes even each other! A full-grown T.rex was about as large as a school bus. They walked upright and had unusually small forelimbs. Despite what is shown in movies, this dinosaur wouldn't be able to chase at high speeds; it's more likely that it moved at a moderately brisk pace.

Size: 12.3 metres; Weight: 16,800 to 28,000 lbs / 7.5 to 12.5 tonnes

Velociraptor

Velociraptors are small, wolf-sized dinosaurs that lived during the Late Cretaceous period. Did you know that the name "velociraptor" means "speedy thief"? Velociraptors actually had feathers. They are like modern-day birds in many aspects and probably hunted just like other birds of prey today.

Size: 1.8 metres; Weight: 100 lbs / 45 kg

Coelophysis

Coelophysis were among the early dinosaurs. Though they were not huge or fierce, they were quick runners and very agile, capable of catching insects and small reptiles. This dinosaur had hollow limbs, making them lightweight and hence capable of moving around quickly.

Size: 7 metres; Weight: 33 lbs / 15 kg

Spinosaurus

Spinosaurus, or "spine lizard", was the biggest known carnivorous dinosaur, and was much larger than T.rex. It had long spines connected to the skin running down its back in an arrangement that is referred to as a "sail". Scientists discovered that they were capable of swimming and very likely spent a considerable time in water.

Size: 4.3 to 7 metres; Weight: Up to 44,000 lbs / 20 tonnes

Diplodocus

Considered to be the longest dinosaur, Diplodocus was a gigantic herbivore with a long neck and a longer tail to balance the weight. It is classified under a group of massive, plant-eating dinosaurs called sauropods. A Diplodocus might be massive, but it was still able to rear up and stand on its hind legs to reach branches of tall trees!

Size: 24 metres long, 5 metres tall; Weight: 22,000 to 35,000 lbs / 10 to 16 tonnes

Stegosaurus

Stegosaurus was another large, herbivorous dinosaur with a characteristic feature – a set of bony plates lining its back and spikes on its tail. This bus-sized dinosaur had a small head with a tiny brain – considered to be about the size of a walnut. The word "stegosaurus" means "roofed lizard" and the plates on its back probably helped in regulating temperature.

Size: 9 metres; Weight: 11,600 to 15,400 lbs / 5.25 to 7 tonnes

Parasaurolophus

A beaked plant-eating dinosaur, parasaurolophus had a prominent head crest consisting of a network of tube-like structures which was capable of producing sounds (like a trumpet) to communicate. The dinosaur's beak helped pluck leaves, just like birds today use them.

Size: 9.5 metres; Weight: 5,400 lbs / 2.5 tonnes